WELCOME TO THE CONSTRUCTION SITE

Knuckleboom Loader

1

Samantha Bell

Published in the United States of America
by Cherry Lake Publishing
Ann Arbor, Michigan
www.cherrylakepublishing.com

Content Adviser: Louis Teel, Professor of Heavy Equipment Operating, Central Arizona College
Reading Adviser: Cecilia Minden, PhD, Literacy expert and children's author

Photo Credits: ©Courtesy of Barko Hydraulics, LLC, cover, 2, 4, 6, 8, 10, 12, 14, 16, 18; ©Dwight Smith / Shutterstock, 20

Library of Congress Cataloging-in-Publication Data
Names: Bell, Samantha, author.
Title: Knuckleboom loader / Samantha Bell.
Description: Ann Arbor : Cherry Lake Publishing, [2018] | Series: Welcome to the construction site | Includes bibliographical references and index. | Audience: Grades K to 3.
Identifiers: LCCN 2018003283| ISBN 9781534129238 (hardcover) | ISBN 9781534132436 (pbk.) | ISBN 9781534130937 (pdf) | ISBN 9781534134133 (hosted ebook)
Subjects: LCSH: Cranes, derricks, etc.—Juvenile literature. | Loaders (Machines)—Juvenile literature.
Classification: LCC TJ1363 .B3788 2018 | DDC 621.8/6—dc23
LC record available at https://lccn.loc.gov/2018003283

Cherry Lake Publishing would like to acknowledge the work of The Partnership for 21st Century Learning. Please visit *www.p21.org* for more information.

Printed in the United States of America
Corporate Graphics

Table of Contents

Why do you think these trees needed to be cut down?

Logging and Cargo

Knuckleboom loaders are **cranes**. They are machines with long arms.

They lift supplies and machinery. They pick up logs using their **grapples**. They move heavy **cargo**.

A knuckleboom loader has two **booms**. The booms open and close like fingers on your hand.

Tight Spaces

The booms can fold in and become smaller. Now the loader is easy to move.

A knuckleboom loader is easy to store. It can work in tight spaces.

Extra Reach

The booms can stretch out and become longer. Now the loader can reach things far away.

Some knuckleboom loaders have a bucket. Some have a grapple.

What jobs could a knuckleboom loader do on a boat?

Many Different Jobs

Some move on wheels or **tracks**. Some are attached to trucks or boats.

Knuckleboom loaders can do many different jobs!

Find Out More

Book

Perritano, John. *Construction Machines*. New York: Gareth
Stevens Publishing, 2014.

Website

Skyco Equipment—Demonstration of a Knuckle Boom
www.skycoequipmentinc.wordpress.com/2012/09/10
/demonstration-of-a-knuckle-boom/
Watch a video showing how a knuckleboom loader works.

Glossary

booms (BOOMZ) the long arms of a crane
cargo (KAHR-go) something carried from one place to another in
a ship, airplane, train, truck, or other vehicle
cranes (KRAYNZ) machines with swinging arms used to lift and
move heavy objects
grapples (GRAP-uhlz) an attachment that can grip or hold things
tracks (TRAKS) the metal or rubber belts on a vehicle that make
it move

Home and School Connection

Use this list of words from the book to help your child become a better reader. Word games and writing activities can help beginning readers reinforce literacy skills.

a	far	loader	store
and	fingers	loaders	stretch
are	fold	logs	supplies
arms	grapple	longer	the
attached	grapples	machines	they
away	hand	many	things
become	has	move	tight
boats	have	now	to
booms	heavy	on	tracks
bucket	in	or	trucks
can	is	out	two
cargo	it	pick	up
cranes	jobs	reach	wheels
different	knuckleboom	smaller	with
do	lift	some	work
easy	like	spaces	

Index

About the Author

Samantha Bell has written and illustrated over 60 books for children. She lives in South Carolina with her family and pets.